THE FALLEN

Story by Mary Ingram
Illustrations by Andrew C. Westling

To my friend and illustrator, Andrew. You unwrapped your potential and discovered the gift of God's grace during your incarceration. Thank you for sharing this journey with me. I am forever blessed to have you in my life.

— Mary

To my loving grandmother Vondell. Without you in my life I would not be who I am today. Your unconditional love was like a life-preserver when I was drowning.

— Andrew

FOREWARD

I am a friend of Andrew, the illustrator for this story. I met him three years ago when he had already been incarcerated for more than 10 years.

The story is about brokenness, chaos, anger, grief and redemption. The story is about being carried along by the events of life when there is no purpose or direction for guidance.

I have received more than 100 letters from Andrew and have spent many hours in conversation with him. He has chosen to share deeply and honestly with me. He revealed to me his life as a young man moving through a chaotic life of one bad decision after another until it ultimately led to prison.

Just as the story of the fallen stick did not end with the stick in the hands of the thief, so also Andrew's story does not end with imprisonment. In the hands of the wise and skillful wood carver, the fallen stick was carved into a beautiful fife. The wood carver, seeing past the rough exterior, envisioned the hidden beauty that lay within the stick.

My hope is that all who read this story will begin to look for the hidden beauty and potential that lay not only within themselves, but also in the lives of those around them.

I hope the reader sees the wisdom in letting go of anger, bitterness, jealousy and guilt. They can stifle and ultimately destroy the potential and beauty that lies within us all.

Andrew is still on a journey. So am I.

I am grateful that our lives have crossed paths. I am proud to call him a friend. I am excited to be a part of what the "Wood Carver" has yet envisioned for Andrew!

— Chris

A strong gust of wind blew through the canopy of the tree,

knocking a branch to the ground.
Once a part of nature's beauty,
the stick was devastated to find itself
lying useless on the ground.

The stick lay there silent,
wondering what will become of it.

Feeling abandoned,

its pain grew into anger.

Its future was now uncertain.

A young lad,
hiking through the countryside,
discovered the stick.

Feeling the weight of the wood in his hand,
the boy tossed a stone into the air and took a mighty swing.

The stick made contact with the stone,
whacking it into a neighboring field.

The brutality made the stick feel powerful.

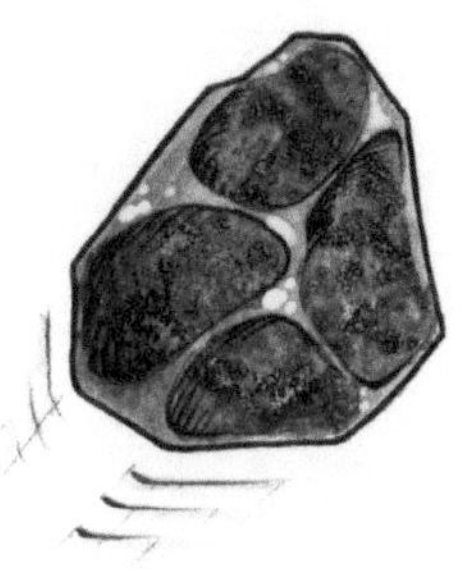

After the assault on several stones,
the boy tired.
He dropped the stick
and continued on his way.

Days later, an old woman
who was out enjoying the fresh air
stumbled upon the stick.

She had been battling
the tall grass on her walk
and thought the stick would serve
as a good weapon against the reeds.

She began striking down the vegetation
with the stick, making her way
through the brush.

When she approached a clearing,
the woman threw down the stick
and proceeded on her journey.

The stick was beginning to think
it had found its calling.

As night fell, a thief passing through spotted the stick.

It gave him an idea.

The thief was envious
of the wealthy merchants in town

and decided to use the stick to assault
one of them and steal his money.

One shop owner was working late
when the thief entered his business.

The gentleman was hard at work
and didn't notice the intruder.

The thief raised the stick and clubbed the man over the head,

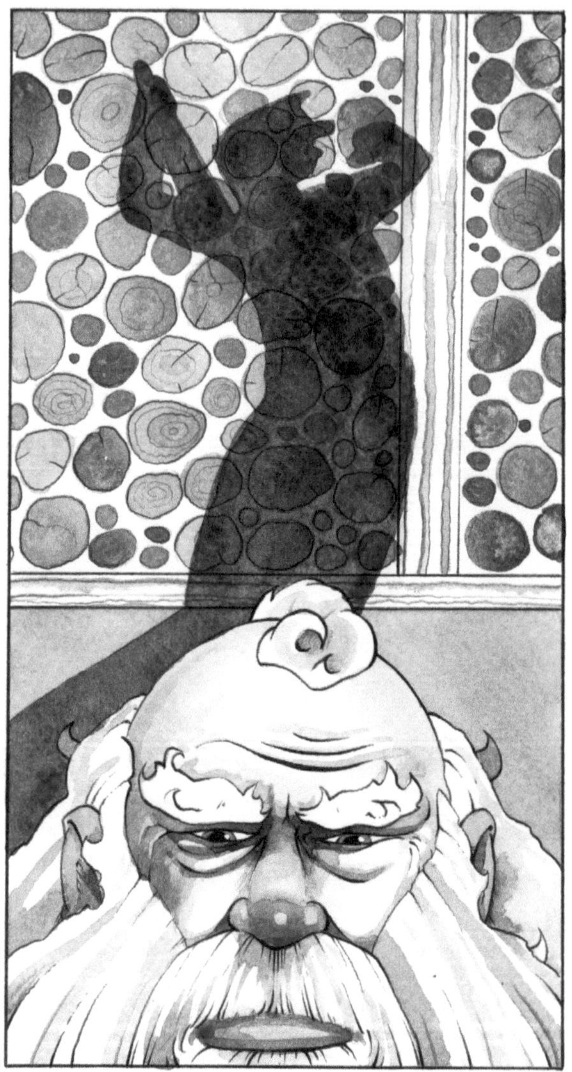

knocking him unconscious.
The thief gathered up the shop owner's fortune
and ran away.

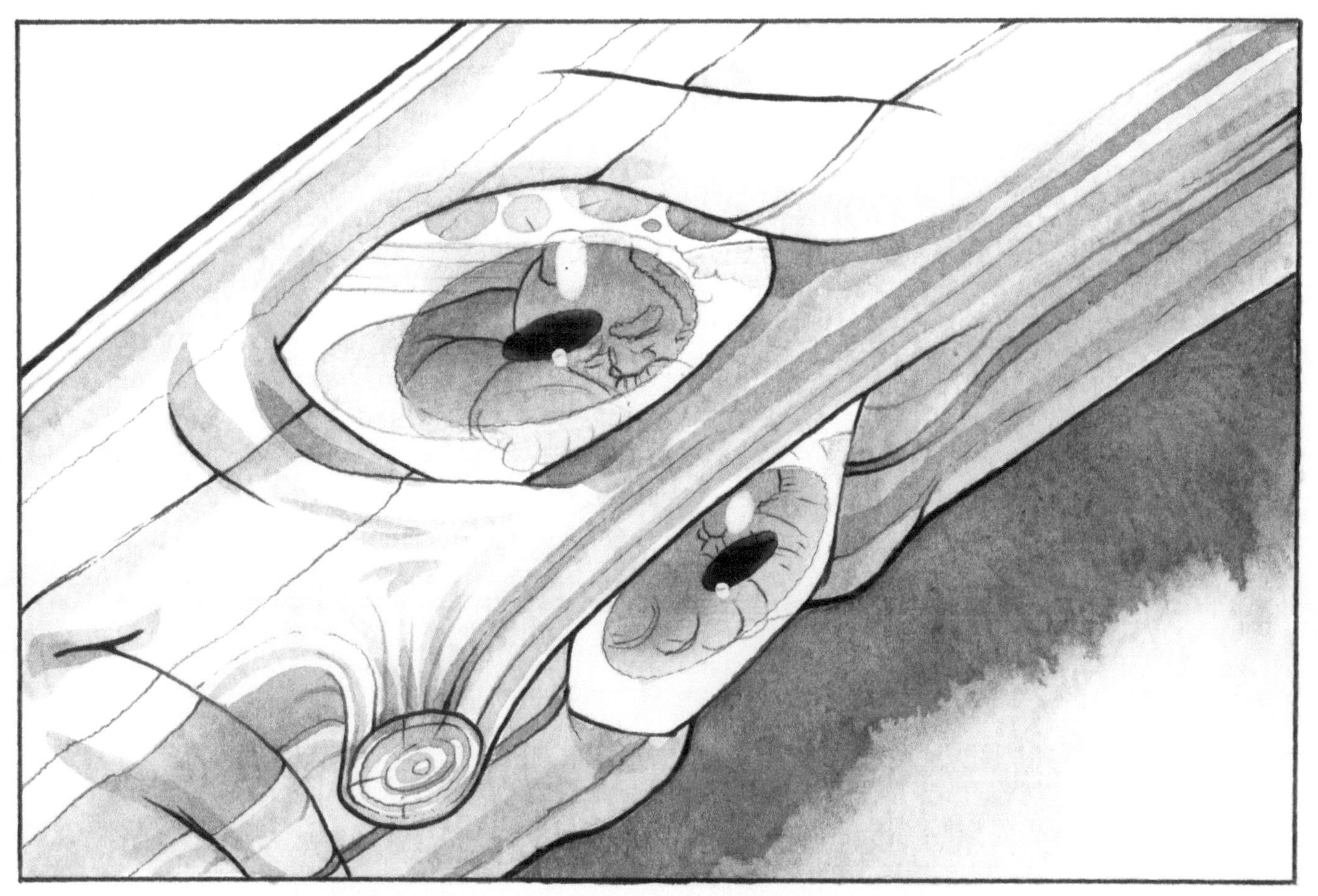

As the stick stared at the beaten man,
it was overwhelmed with the feeling of shame
for what it had become: a weapon of hate.

Stained with the shop owner's blood,
the stick asked itself:
"What has led me to display such violence?"

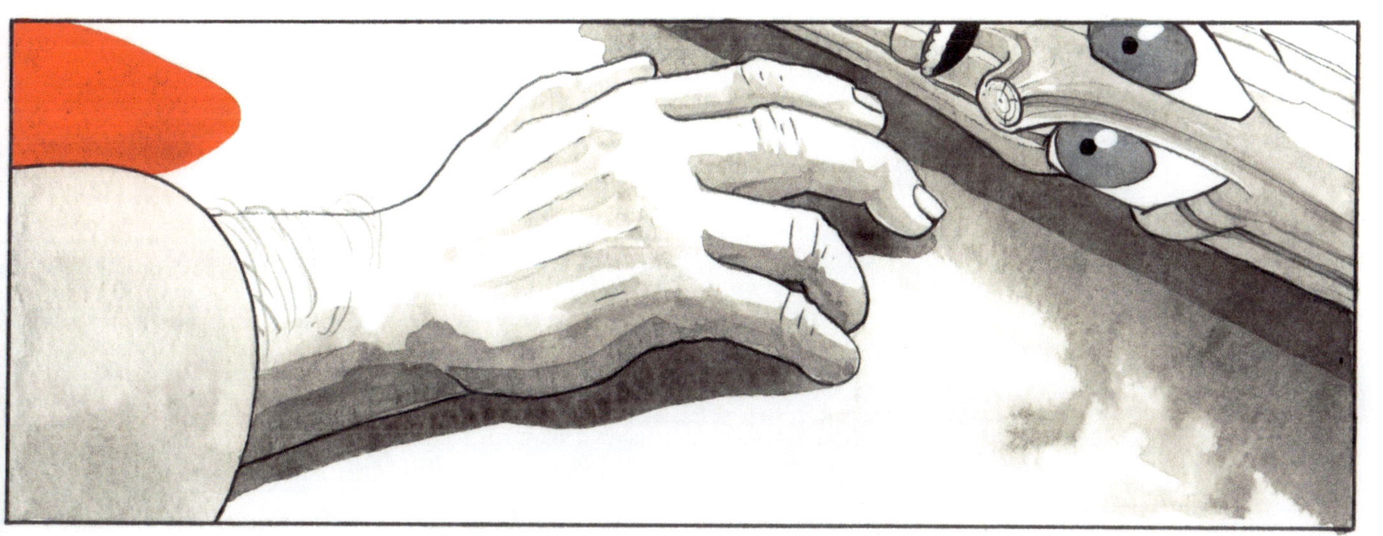

When the man awoke, he was stunned
and unable to rise quickly.

Once his vision cleared,

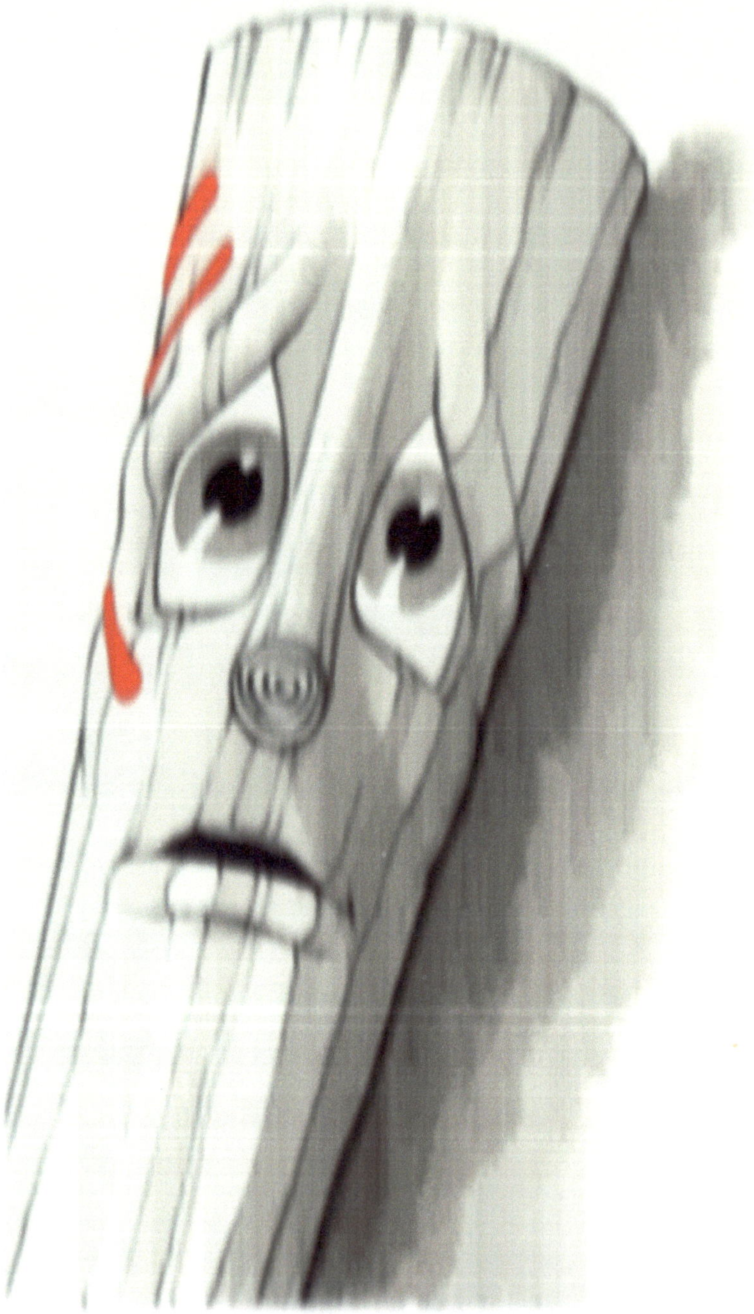

he saw the stick.

The man took the stick and used it as a cane to get to his feet.
The stick felt the shop owner's secure grip
and did its best to steady him.
Together they made their way to a small stool
where the man could rest.

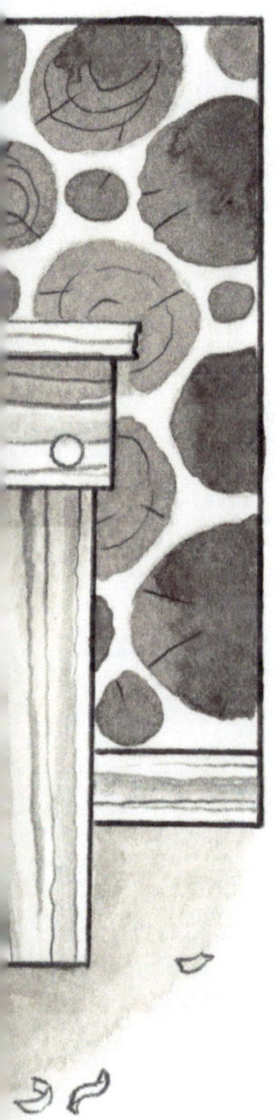

It was then that the man realized the stick's role in the attack.

He reached for a cloth and tried to wipe the blood away.

The stick wept.

The man examined the stick closely
and saw beauty and potential in it.
The man, a master at his trade,
began to chisel away the rough old wood
to expose the grains deep within.

The stick asked, "Is it possible
to become more than I am?"

The man smiled.
*"When you embrace all your imperfections,
you will find beauty,"* he explained.

"You are enough."

When the man completed his work,
the stick had been transformed
into a beautiful wooden fife.

It has become what it was intended for ...

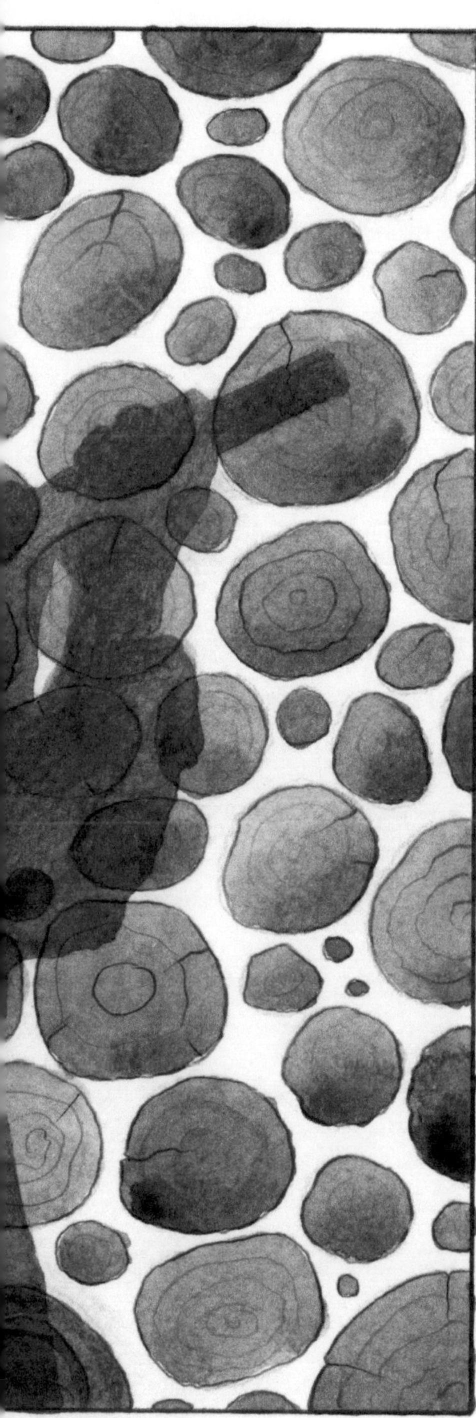

... an instrument of beauty and peace.

MISSION STATEMENT

The story was written to honor the memory of victims of violent crimes and help heal the hurt for so many families. It is nearly impossible to imagine the pain they feel when they lose a loved one to violence. Hearts shatter. Lives are forever changed. Is forgiveness even possible?

It was also written to embrace the offenders who must come to terms with their past actions and find some way to move forward in such a way that will bring honor back to their lives.

We pray this message of love will reach the families whose lives were altered by violent crimes It is not intended to re-aggravate a heartache, but to share the burden of their pain.

Net proceeds from this book will be given to juvenile programs and programs supporting victim/offender initiatives.

ABOUT THE AUTHOR

Mary Ingram is a gardener with a pen and a voice. She has devoted her life to serving children as a coach, volunteer, juvenile justice coordinator, parent and grandparent. She possesses a strong belief in community service and encourages others to play their role in making the world a better place. While working on her first children's book, she discovered her illustrator behind bars at the Lincoln Correctional Center in Lincoln, Nebraska. After corresponding with Andrew through several letters, followed by a face-to-face meeting, she was compelled to write The Fallen. It was her gift to him.

Acknowledgments:

With deepest gratitude, I want to thank everyone who believed in this project. To my brother, Charles, you tell me I can do anything and make me believe I am enough.

To my daughters. To my oldest daughter, you're always there to listen and help me clarify my thoughts, and to my youngest daughter, I am grateful to you for sharing your talents of editing and masterfully combining the illustrations with the words to create The Fallen.

The story was brought to life with the video skills of Ivanhoe. Thank you for your contribution as it helps us share the story with the world.

To Mike, for sharing your artistic impression while creating the book cover.

To my best friend and confidante, Cheryl. You know the best and worst of me and love me all the same. Everyone should have such a friend.

To my nephew, Craig. You loved and accepted everyone who crossed your path. Your spirit lives on in each of us.

In March 1998, eighteen year old Andrew C. Westling was living in Omaha, Nebraska when he was arrested and convicted of a violent crime where a young man lost his life. Distraught, addicted to drugs and alcohol, he sat in a jail cell sobering up- evaluating the path that led to perdition. He sought to remedy his destructive choices. Confronted with the reality of his actions, there were two directions to choose from- life in prison or the possibility of parole. Deciding to be more than he had become, striving to reach some level of atonement, he made up his mind to turn his life around.

Acknowledgments:

My heartfelt thanks to Mary for believing in me and providing this opportunity.

Thanks to my family and friends, you inspire me to reach beyond my grasp.

A special thanks to Chris and his family for your support and fellowship. And thanks to all of you who have encouraged me over the years, without your expectations I would fall short of my own.

And most importantly: Thank you Lord for shining your grace on my life, for opening my heart and mind to your truth and allowing me to have just one more day to make amends for my destructive past. I thank you, for everything is possible through faith in You.

For those not named, you know I love you and thank you too.

When Mary first presented me with this story, it made my heart clinch and my eyes well. Not because it drew parallels to my past, but because it reminded me that no matter how we fail in life, it is never too late to become who you should've always been!

I believe in God's will, his purpose for my life and it is that faith and understanding that strengthens me. This truth propels me forward from my past perdition and drives me to be everything I wasn't the night so much was lost.

This story reminds me that through the blood that Christ shed, I am saved. That I am transformed. That I can be more, through God's grace...I am forgiven.

Thank you for sharing in this story. If you have any questions or concerns please contact me through The Fallen Fan Page on Facebook.

— Andrew C. Westling

9 781470 013486